WORMS

Nature's FRIENDS

by Joyce Markovics

NORWOOD HOUSE PRESS

NORWOOD HOUSE 🏠 PRESS

For more information about Norwood House Press, please visit our website at: www.norwoodhousepress.com or call 866-565-2900.

Book Designer: Ed Morgan
Editorial and Production: Bowerbird Books

Photo Credits: freepik.com, cover; © iStock.com/brittak, title page; © iStock.com/iso100k, 4; © Beverley Van Praagh, 5; © Beverley Van Praagh, 6; Public Domain, 7; Wikimedia Commons, 8; Maximilian Paradiz/flickr, 9; © iStock.com/motorolka, 10; © Steve Shinn, 11; © iStock.com/Hennadii, 12; schizoform/flickr, 13; © iStock.com/jlmcloughlin, 14; © iStock.com/neenawat, 15 top; freepik.com, 15 bottom; © iStock.com/I love take a photo, 16; © iStock.com/Ashley-Belle Burns, 18; freepik.com, 19; © iStock.com/Zummolo, 20; freepik.com, 21; © iStock.com/Tramper2, 22; Wikimedia Commons, 23; Billy Freeman/Unsplash.com, 24; © iStock.com/Brian Brown, 25 top; freepik.com, 25 bottom; freepik.com, 26; © iStock.com/zianlob, 29.

Hardcover ISBN: 978-1-68450-763-4
Paperback ISBN: 978-1-68404-780-2

Library of Congress Cataloging-in-Publication Data

Names: Markovics, Joyce L., author.
Title: Worms / by Joyce Markovics.
Description: Chicago : Norwood House Press, [2023] | Series:
   Nature's friends | Includes bibliographical references and index. |
   Audience: Grades 2-3
Identifiers: LCCN 2021061075 (print) | LCCN 2021061076 (ebook) | ISBN
   9781684507634 (hardcover) | ISBN 9781684047802 (paperback) | ISBN
   9781684047864 (ebook)
Subjects: LCSH: Worms--Juvenile literature.
Classification: LCC QL386.6 .M37 2023 (print) | LCC QL386.6 (ebook) | DDC
   592/.3--dc23/eng/20220106
LC record available at https://lccn.loc.gov/2021061075
LC ebook record available at https://lccn.loc.gov/2021061076

353N—082022

Manufactured in the United States of America in North Mankato, Minnesota.

CONTENTS

UNDERGROUND SOUND

It's a spring day in Gippsland, Australia. Gurgling noises come from a wet patch of soil. They're followed by what sounds like water draining from a bathtub. Deep underground, a giant creature is on the move. It's often heard but rarely seen. The animal has no arms, legs, or eyes. What is it? It's a giant Gippsland earthworm.

This big earthworm ranges from 3 feet (0.9 m) to as long as a small car! The worm has a grayish-blue body and a purple head. Gippsland earthworms make their homes in moist soil along stream banks. There, they dig tunnels called burrows in which they live. Because they're so big, they can be heard sloshing through their burrows. These worms seldom leave the soil unless heavy rain floods them out.

A giant Gippsland earthworm

The longest earthworm in the world was found in South Africa. It was 21 feet (6.7 m) in length!

Scientist Beverley Van Praagh loves big worms. In fact, she has been studying giant Gippsland earthworms for more than 25 years. "They live underground and have so many secrets," Beverley says. "They're just fascinating." Beverley is one of only a few people in the world to hold the giant worm. "They feel cold and slippery," she says.

Scientist Beverley Van Praagh holds a giant Gippsland earthworm that has been flooded out of its burrow. She's careful not to hurt the delicate animal.

Beverley believes Australian farmers first noticed the mega worm in the 1870s. "They actually thought it was a snake," she says. At that time, the worms were **abundant**. One early story tells of farmers plowing the land. "The fields would be red with blood from these worms," says Beverley. "They would hang from the plows like spaghetti." Since then, the Gippsland earthworm **population** has crashed. Beverley is hard at work to help this special worm before time runs out.

This image shows early farmers in Australia.

In 2012, the Australian government made a law to protect giant Gippsland earthworms.

ALL ABOUT WORMS

Worms are invertebrates (in-VUR-tuh-brits). Unlike people, they don't have a backbone or a skeleton. Most worms have long, thin bodies and no legs. They tend to live in water or other moist places. Some worms are as tiny as the period at the end of this sentence. Others, like the giant Gippsland, can be huge. There are many varieties of worms, including earthworms.

The longest worm of any kind is the bootlace worm. It lives in the sea. This worm can stretch more than 180 feet (55 m) long!

The giant Gippsland is one of more than 3,800 kinds of earthworms. Earthworms got their name because they often live in the soil. Not only do earthworms come in many sizes, but they also come in different colors. These colors range from pink to red to green. Earthworms fit into three main groups, depending on where they live in the soil: leaf litter dwellers, soil dwellers, and deep burrowers. Some dwell in dead leaves on the soil. Others live within the top foot or so of the soil. The final group lives as much as 10 feet (3 m) underground. They dig burrows in the soil that look like tiny elevator shafts.

The soil-eating green earthworm has a natural greenish-blue color. What also sets it apart are three sucker-like disks on its body.

The best-known deep burrower is the common earthworm. This pinkish-brown worm can grow up to 14 inches (36 cm) long. It can be as thick as a pencil. Common earthworms are found in North America, Europe, and Asia. They're also very plentiful. For every square foot of soil, there may be ten common earthworms.

The common earthworm's head is often darker than its tail.

Common earthworms' bodies are made up of about 100 ringlike parts called segments, or annuli (AN-yuh-lahy). Covering the annuli are tiny bristles known as setae (SET-ay). Worms use their setae to anchor themselves in the soil. To move, earthworms have muscles in their segments. These muscles form a ring around their bodies. As the muscles tighten and relax, they help the worms move.

This close-up view shows an earthworm's setae.

Earthworms don't just have one heart. They have five! However, their "hearts" are more like special blood vessels.

How do common earthworms breathe in the soil? They take in air through their skin! To do this, earthworms have to be moist. Wet soil helps. But the mucus their skin makes is crucial. This slimy substance coats the worms' bodies. It keeps them extra moist. The moisture allows gases such as oxygen in the soil to pass through the worms' wet skin.

Even though earthworms don't have eyes, they can sense light from dark.

If you looked at a cross section of the soil, you would see lots of wriggling worms.

If a worm's skin dries out, it wouldn't be able to breathe and would die.

Earthworms are also **adapted** to feed underground. They eat soil, which is full of rotting leaves and other dead matter. Every earthworm has a small mouth but no teeth. After it finds and swallows its food, special muscles push the food into a body part called the crop. Then the food enters a **gizzard**. The gizzard contains tiny stones that grind up the food. Then the food passes into the **intestine** where it's taken in by the worm's body. Finally, waste called castings passes out of the worm's backside.

SOIL MAKERS

As earthworms tunnel through the soil, they transform it! Their wriggly bodies create small openings in the soil. These pockets hold water and air. Both of these things help the roots of plants grow. Worm burrows also allow water to drain through the soil. Plants with deep roots, such as some trees, benefit from this. Also, when earthworms move, they mix different layers of the soil. This **enriches** the soil.

This earthworm is sliding through wet soil.

Worm castings on a lawn

In addition, the castings that earthworms make are a great **fertilizer**. They are full of **nutrients**. Plants use these nutrients to grow big and strong. Many of these plants provide food, such as vegetables and fruits, for people. Castings also soften the soil so roots can more easily grow.

You've probably seen worm castings on a lawn. They look like tiny piles of poop!

Worms can eat their weight in soil each day. Think about how much food it would be if you ate your weight in sandwiches!

Despite their small size, earthworms help nature in a big way. Let's say there are 500,000 worms in 1 acre (0.4 ha) of soil. Together, these worms can make 50 tons (45 metric tons) of castings. That's a lot of fertilizer! Picture 100,000 metal coffee cans filled with castings.

Those same worms can also create miles of burrows in the soil. These burrows equal 2,000 feet (609 m) of 6-inch (15 cm) drainage pipe. The burrows could help stop a yard from flooding during a rainstorm.

Earthworms have another amazing ability. They can regrow lost segments.

WORM COMPOST

Many people make use of worms' amazing abilities. They use worms for composting! Composting turns food scraps into a rich fertilizer called compost. The worms eat leftover vegetables and fruits. Then the scraps pass through the worms' bodies. The compost that comes out of the worms can be used to grow new plants.

The top photo shows food scraps before worms turned them into compost (bottom photo).

Worm composting, or vermicomposting, is popular around the world. Some people set up composters in their backyards. To do this, they use plastic or wood containers. These are often filled with strips of moist newspaper. To thrive, worms need a damp, dark place to live. They also need plenty of food scraps. After feeding the worms for three to five months, the compost will be ready to **harvest**!

Farmer holding compost with worms

People often use red worms, also known as red wigglers, in their worm composters.

People with small farms also use worms to make compost. They live in places such as China, Cuba, India, and the United States. Worm compost helps farmers create healthier soil and better crops. Instead of having to buy food, they're able to grow more food for themselves. Some small farmers grow so much food, they can sell it to make a profit.

A worm farmer holding a bunch of worms

A scientist checking the quality of soil

Scientists are still not sure why worm compost is so beneficial. However, they are busy collecting data about it. A scientist in Hawaii has found that tomatoes, strawberries, and grapes produce thirty percent more fruit when grown with vermicompost. Vermicompost can also improve the quality of soil in areas with poor soil. Experts are looking into ways worms can help make barren land fertile.

FOOD FOR OTHERS

Many animals—big and small—dine on earthworms. Larger animals include skunks, foxes, snakes, and badgers. Moles, frogs, salamanders, and snails are smaller critters that hunt and eat worms. Even tinier animals, such as some beetles, eat worms. Birds, too, love worms. You've probably seen a robin tugging an earthworm from the ground. An adult robin can eat 14 feet (4.3 m) of earthworms in one day!

A mole gobbles up an earthworm.

In southern Venezuela, the Ye'kuana people gather worms for food. Then they gut and cook them. The worms are a nutritious part of their diet. The Ye'kuana aren't the only worm eaters. People in New Zealand and China eat worms as a special treat. What do earthworms taste like? They taste a little like what they eat—soil!

The Ye'kuana people get most of their food from the forests and rivers where they live.

23

UNDER THREAT

This large machine is clearing the land to make room for new houses.

Earthworms are under threat. Why? Much of the healthy soil around the world is gone. People have cleared the land to make room for new houses and farms. This can cause erosion, which wears away soil. Some experts think that half of the planet's soil has already eroded. Farmers also threaten earthworms by **tilling** the soil. For example, when soil is plowed, many worms can be chopped up and killed in the process.

Planes called crop dusters spray pesticides on crops.

Humans have also polluted the soil with **toxic** materials. Pesticides, for example, are one of the greatest risks to worms. People apply these poisons to their lawns and crops to kill pests. However, some pesticides are deadly to worms.

Healthy soil is needed to grow ninety-five percent of the foods people eat.

A WORLD WITHOUT WORMS

What if there were no earthworms? Earthworms are a **critical** part of the soil and the **ecosystem**. Without them, the soil would be far less fertile. Plants would struggle to grow. It would be difficult for farmers to grow crops. In addition, a variety of worm-eating animals would have less food.

Scientist Beverley Van Praagh is working hard to help save worms, especially the giant Gippsland earthworm. Tilling and toxins have pushed them close to **extinction**. Beverley is educating farmers about ways they can help the big worms. As she says, "The giant Gippsland earthworm cannot recover easily from changes to their environment." Beverley hopes there's still time to make a difference.

Earthworms squirming close to the surface of the soil

EARTHWORM EXPERIMENT!

Earthworms are specially adapted for living and feeding underground. Learn about earthworms by carefully examining one!

- With an adult's help, get a small tray, a wet paper towel, and some gardening gloves.

- On a warm day, go outside with your adult helper and find an earthworm in the soil.

- Gently place the earthworm on the wet paper towel on the tray. Observe it. How does it move?

- Get a dry paper towel and place it next to the wet one. Gently stretch the worm so half its body is on the dry paper towel and half is on the wet one. Does the worm prefer to be on one side or the other? Do you think the worm can sense moisture? Why or why not?

- Finally, return the worm to the same spot where you found it outside.

HAVE FUN OBSERVING A WORM!

GLOSSARY

abundant (uh-BUHN-duhnt): a great quantity.

adapted (uh-DAP-tid): changed over time to be fit for the environment.

anchor (ANG-kur): to hold in place.

barren (BAR-uhn): unable to grow plants or produce crops.

blood vessels (BLUHD VESS-uhlz): tiny tubes, such as veins, that carry blood around a person's or an animal's body.

critical (KRIT-uh-kuhl): very important.

drainage (DREY-nij): the act of removing surplus water.

ecosystem (EE-koh-siss-tuhm): a community of animals and plants that depend on one another to live.

enriches (en-RICH-uhs): makes better or increases in quality.

extinction (ek-STINGK-shuhn): when a type of animal or plant dies out completely.

fertile (FUR-tuhl): capable of producing lots of plants such as crops.

fertilizer (FUR-tuh-lize-ur): a substance added to soil to help plants grow.

gizzard (GIZ-erd): a pouch in the stomach of some animals that grinds food using small stones.

harvest (HAR-vist): to collect or gather crops.

intestine (in-TESS-tin): the long, tube-shaped part on the inside of an animal's body where food is turned into fuel and waste.

nutrients (NOO-tree-uhnts): substances needed by animals and plants to grow and stay healthy.

oxygen (AHK-suh-juhn): an invisible gas found in water or air, which people and animals breathe.

population (pop-yuh-LAY-shuhn): the number of people or animals living in a place.

substance (SUHB-stuhns): a particular kind of matter.

tilling (TIL-ing): preparing land for crops.

toxic (TOK-sik): poisonous or deadly.

FOR MORE INFORMATION

Books

Kalman, Bobbie. *The Life Cycle of an Earthworm*. New York, NY: Crabtree Publishing, 2003.
Read about earthworms from birth to adulthood.

Loewen, Nancy. *Garden Wigglers*. Minneapolis, MN: Picture Window Books, 2005.
This book explores earthworms in your backyard.

Waters, Kate. *Curious about Worms*. New York, NY: Grosset & Dunlap, 2017.
Discover fascinating facts about different types of worms.

Websites

BioKIDS: Earthworms
(http://www.biokids.umich.edu/critters/Oligochaeta/)
Read about worm basics.

National Geographic Kids: Earthworm
(https://kids.nationalgeographic.com/animals/invertebrates/facts/earthworm)
Find out about earthworms.

University of Illinois Extension: Worm Facts
(https://web.extension.illinois.edu/worms/facts/)
Readers can learn amazing worm facts.

INDEX

ABOUT THE AUTHOR

Joyce Markovics has written hundreds of books for kids. She thinks worms are wonderful. Joyce lives in an old, creaky house along the Hudson River. She hopes the readers of this book will take action—in small and big ways—to protect nature, one of our greatest gifts. Joyce would like to thank Beverley Van Praagh and Adrian Wackett for contributing to this book.